Printed in the USA
CPSIA information can be obtained
at www.ICGtesting.com
LVHW020448271123
765003LV00013B/965

9 781090 863027